Two under Two:

How to Survive and Not Kill Your Husband

Danielle Lacourse Vaughn

ISBN: 9781082107962 (paperback)

For every mom who wonders
if she's doing it right.

You are.

I think.

Intro

They say you write best when you write about what you know. For me, that's parenting. Or at least trying. After having two kids in under two years, I've learned a lot, cried a ton, and have used more undereye concealer than is considered normal for someone my age. This job, creating and raising little humans, is no joke. Unless you're Amy Schumer and just give birth to eighteen years' worth of material.

It's funny how life works—you can live thirty years of your life establishing who you are and how you define yourself. And then nine months, a bout of hemorrhoids, and a few perineal tears later, the game has changed. You have changed. Forever. *Twice.* You are living at the will of a toddler and a newborn, and your priorities have shifted. Shower? Maybe later. Coffee? Reheated in the microwave at least a dozen times before noon. Sitting down to eat? Now I'm just laughing. And peeing. Because that's our reality now.

I understand time is limited. So much so that this whole thing was written on my iPhone while the kids were sleeping. I also know that reading a book isn't at the top of your ever-growing to-do list. I get it. But the truth is, I'm not really a writer and this isn't really a book. You see, I'm a nurse. I enjoy helping other people and am empathetic at my core. Yet, my whole life I've felt compelled to write. I have written and rewritten various story lines over the years but have never felt connected enough to the material. Until now.

It's time to take a break from scrolling through photos of your kids because the nurse in me wants to help the mom in you.

Seriously, stop. You just put them to bed.

If You're Reading This

If you're reading this, it's not a self-help book, and I'm not telling you what to do.

If you're reading this, I honestly don't know how I got so lucky. I have two healthy kids, a supportive husband, and an app on my phone that delivers alcohol.

If you're reading this, I can't help you sleep train your baby, organize your closet, find your love language, or discipline your toddler.

If you're reading this, I know I'm not the only one to have two under two. Many people have many more, and I don't know how they do it. Seriously, how? At the end of the day, I'm half expecting to receive a Nobel Peace Prize for my outstanding work in Sibling Rivalry.

If you're reading this, I love my kids. Obviously.

If you're reading this, the word "husband" is an umbrella term. It can mean your partner, spouse, or significant other. You know, the person you nag to empty the dishwasher. Yes, that one.

If you're reading this, I'm not claiming to be a literary genius or to be even remotely good at writing. I write how I speak, and when I do, I'm almost always dropping my *r*'s. I'd like to blame it on my Rhode Island accent, but in reality, it's probably some combination of Mom Brain, an overdose of kombucha, and a little bit of toddler-induced CTE.

If you're reading this, I love my husband. Maybe not so obviously.

If you're reading this, you need to know that I'm a stay-at-home mom. That means I'm lucky enough to work this twenty-four-hour shift that makes my former job in the operating room look like a lazy Sunday brunch with the girls. You know what needs to go on my résumé? This shit. You know what can't go on my résumé? This shit.

If you're reading this, I hope you can have at least one solo trip to the bathroom today. Because I didn't.

And finally—

If you're reading this and your husband is still alive, my job here is done.

Two Under Two

These past twelve months have been busy. *Very* busy. Not only is my infant adjusting to a world outside the womb, my toddler is still very much a baby, and my husband and I are now almost exclusively communicating in dirty looks and resentful side glances. Somewhere between the Fourth of July and Christmas, we entered a primitive state of survival. Eat, change their diapers, pray they sleep. Repeat.

In an attempt to make your passage through the baby dark ages a bit brighter, I have created a guide. So take a deep breath, grab your cup of cold coffee, and enjoy.

#1

Sleep Like a Baby

You had another baby. Congratulations! The upside? You get to snuggle and stare in complete awe while they sleep soundly on your chest. The downside? You're up all night feeding, rocking, changing, and praying that they will fall somewhere in that very small percentile of newborns who learn to sleep through the night. Unfortunately, "Sleep when the baby sleeps" only works when you have one child at home and consume a minimal amount of caffeine. However, you will be able to take advantage of your toddler's nap. Lie down with the baby and try to sleep. For the rest of the day, newborn naps are usually spent cleaning, chasing your toddler, and hoping they don't wake the baby that's now strapped to your chest. Around the four-month mark, your new babe will start going to bed around 7:00–8:00 p.m. and so should you. As marvelous as Mrs. Maisel is, she can wait.

#2

Agriculture and Waste Removal

My husband and I divided up the nighttime duties a long time ago. I feed, he diapers. That way you're a team, and there is less resentment come morning. I mean, he still doesn't have boobs. But it's a start.

#3

To Toss or Not to Toss?

Throw. Shit. Away. Seriously! Go all Marie Kondo on your place, one room at a time. Keep it simple, keep it organized, and keep it up. I promise you don't need all that Tupperware or the underwear from ten years ago that you couldn't fit your postpartum vagina into even if you tried. There. I said it.

#4

Meal Prep 101

With two kids there is more to do and less time to do it. Plain and simple. Remember when you used to meal prep for that diet you were on five years ago? Well, now you're doing it on a grander scale. I make a point to meal prep a few staple items on a weekly basis. Whether it's steel-cut oatmeal, hard-boiled eggs, chicken, fish, pasta, steamed vegetables, or quinoa—it's ready. And so is my toddler. The kid can eat.

#5

Work Out the Workouts

Not being able to work out is a major point of contention in our relationship. Therefore, we made a schedule so we can prioritize our health and get the hell out of the house for an hour. I've always preferred the morning, so I take the 6:00 a.m. slot before the house is awake. Also, make it a full-body workout. I personally love Sculpt at CorePower. It's a heated, weighted sixty-minute yoga class that strengthens your core and helps you sweat out all that wine from the night before. Because you'll need wine. Added bonus? Yoga will help keep you present when playing with your kids and calm when you find your husband's socks on the floor adjacent to, but not in, the hamper. Again.

#6

Strap On

ERGO? Solly? MOBY? Yes, to all! Invest in a few baby carriers so you can be hands free while you play with your toddler. I suggest one for the bottom of the stroller, one in the house, and one in the car. This is especially necessary in the first six months. Not only do you look like a total badass, but it hides the postpartum kangaroo pouch that I know we all love. And don't go hogging all the fun. Get your husband used to wearing it too. Favorites? The Solly for months zero to six and the ERGO for months six to twelve. Find your favorites. Buy. Them. Now.

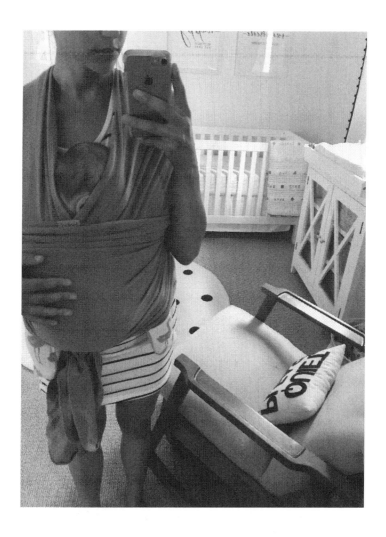

#7

Boob Tube

Ever wonder how moms are able to feed their noise-sensitive infants when a screaming toddler is in the house? It's called TV. They won't talk about it because they're mom-shamed into raising screen-free children, but you need to do what you need to do. Trust me, ten minutes of *Baby Einstein* isn't a gateway to *Narcos*. So give yourself a break. Pick a few short educational shows, and rest easy knowing that we all do it at some point or another. Besides, who are we kidding? All of these organic, no-TV-time, everybody-wins children are going to turn into GMO-eating, binge-watching capitalists anyway.

#8

Mealtime Mayhem

When the baby is ready for table food, you're going to be busy. At this time we introduced the booster seat and passed down the high chair. At the speed with which you need to prepare dinner, you're going to feel like you're a short order cook during lunch hour. My advice? Have busy food. This is food they can munch on while you're reheating their already meal-prepped dinner. Whether it's Puffs, yogurt, or fruit, it keeps them content and buys you some time. Also, watch the floor. Your baby will want to put your toddler's meal remains in their itty-bitty mouths. So keep your eyes open, a broom handy, and accept the fact that you'll probably be eating most of it off the floor at some point.

#9

Pour Mommy

"I like wine," said every mom ever. But I also like not having a hangover. Therefore, I drink organic red wine and limit myself to one glass. Or two if bath time turned into more of a time-out session. Because I'm a stay-at-home mom, I think of Monday–Friday like a workweek and try not to drink on those nights. Keyword: try.

#10

Cover Up

And I don't mean just for your undereye circles. I'm going on year three of a bad hair day, and if it weren't for a baseball cap, I would be mom-shamed right off the playground. Also, invest in three pairs of cheap but trendy sunglasses, and keep them in the diaper bag or stroller. One for your toddler to keep busy with while you're getting out the door. One for your baby to use as a teether because Sophie the Giraffe was apparently a waste of money. And one for you to hide all of your eye rolling while your toddler demands to have the orange sippy cup instead of the blue one.

#11

Get Loaded

One load, every night. I'm talking laundry, people. I grew up in a household that praised cleanliness and all things washed. Now that I'm a mom, I get it. Not only do I operate more efficiently in a clean environment, but when the laundry pile is managed, I feel much less hostile. See? He's still alive. For now. Also, get your husband involved and fold the laundry together after the kids go down. Talk about your day, reconnect, and try not to micromanage his folding skills. Again, keyword: try.

#12

Containment

If your toddler is anything like mine, you have your hands full. You see, my son isn't the sit-in-his-room-and-play quiet type. He's more of the if-it's-too-quiet-then-I'm-worried-he's-holding-his-sister-hostage-for-snack-negotiation type. My husband and I half joke that we will consider ourselves a parental success if by eighteen he is 1) alive, and 2) not incarcerated. You should see him in time-out. It's scary. The kid does time well. With that said, we contain him. Now this doesn't mean he's not having fun, doesn't have the choice to get up, or that this is a so-cial services situation. But if I have to nurse my daughter, bring in groceries, or fold the laundry without him decorating the house with my very large postpartum underwear, then we put him in his booster seat. For a limited amount of time, he sits there with stickers, Play-Doh, puzzles, or any other fine motor skill builder of his choice. Best of all, he loves it. He gets time away from his sister and can create modernized prison shanks with environmentally friendly Play-Doh. I'm kidding. I hope.

#13

Nice Stems

The one consistent piece of advice I have given my pregnant friends is to buy postpartum-support leggings. But not just any legging, the Mother Tucker Leggings by Belly Bandit. Why? They'll help decrease postpartum swelling, make you feel like you've been doing sit-ups instead of eating your toddler's chicken tenders, and they're available on Amazon. Also, invest in a pair of high-rise jeans. I personally love Madewell's 10-inch button front. It's like wearing a built-in corset, and the dark denim wash hides the purée splatter that's destined to be there soon.

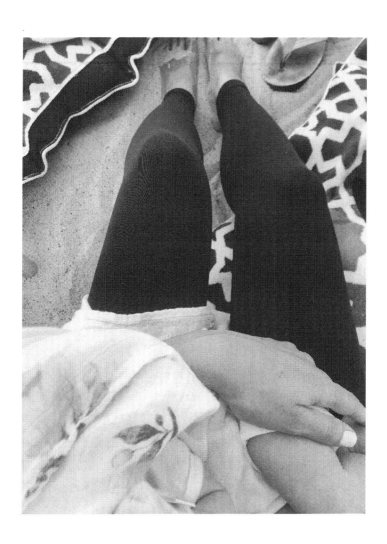

#14

Black Turtleneck

Steve Jobs was on to something. You see, the less thought he put into making mundane decisions like choosing a shirt, the more thought he could put into something else. Like creating that piece of plastic that's glued to your hand. My advice? Start black turtlenecking your meals. Monday through Friday, have one or two options for each meal and snack. Make it healthy and make it a habit, because you won't have the time or energy to run off a box of Oreos at the gym anymore.

#15

F·R·I·E·N·D·S

Momming is hard. But making mom friends is harder. Especially with two kids. You're trying to coordinate different nap and feeding times with this other person who has their own schedule. Most of the time you make plans to break plans. Not intentionally, of course, but you have kids and shit happens. Literally. The key is to keep trying. Send the text, go to the park, meet for coffee, and just try. Not only can they hold your baby when your toddler makes a full sprint toward a moving car, but you can bond over how much you might resent your husband during the hours of 11 p.m.–6 a.m. Because chances are you probably do.

#16

Get the *F* Out of Dodge

Leave. Leave the house. You won't get many of these opportunities, so jump on them when you get the chance. During the week, I almost never get out alone. Seriously. My daughter comes with me to the hair salon, the dentist, is on a first-name basis with my manicurist, and even had to be nursed in the euthanasia room when we put down our cat. So you better believe that on the weekends when my husband is home, I leave. Pedicure? Yes. Facial? Yup. Leisurely grocery shopping without kids while sipping a latte and reading US Weekly? You bet!

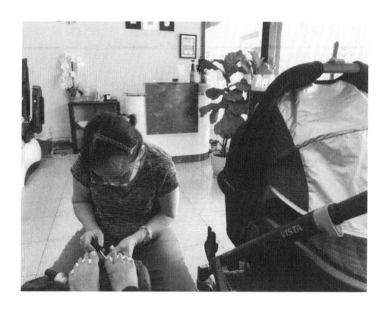

#17

Waitress Wisdom

In college, I used to waitress. The money was good, the bartender was cute, and the drinks were free. Perfect. What I didn't know was that it would make me a more efficient mom one day. How, you ask? Because every waitress knows you never leave a room empty handed and you always have to anticipate what the customer needs next. Except now the customers are your children and the children don't tip. Regardless, find your inner waitress, pick up as you go, and start thinking ten steps ahead. Maybe your house will be cleaner, maybe your day will run smoother, and maybe you'll get the chance to eighty-six your husband.

#18

Shoe Showdown

I'm that weird mom that doesn't allow shoes inside. Unless you're a guest. I always thought it was a little unsanitary and grew up in a no-shoes-on kind of house. But after having kids, it became a strict rule. Not only is it better for your baby that will eventually be crawling, but it extends time between floor washing.

#19

Before You Go

Getting two young kids out of the house by yourself is a living nightmare. In the beginning, it was rough. My son would be running around the house clutching a toilet wand while I was busy handling my daughter's latest blowout. Meanwhile, we were ten minutes late for a playdate, and my caffeine had officially worn off. Now, I prep. Before I leave, I make sure the snacks, diapers, sippy cups, toys, and bottles are in the stroller before they are. To save extra time, make sure to pack the diaper bag the night before.

#20

Controlled Substances

There is nothing scarier than a toddler holding a permanent marker. Hands down. Therefore, put all the crayons, markers, Play-Doh, paint, and pencils in a toddler-proof container. When ready to use, put your toddler in their booster seat or high chair. That way the mess is contained and your walls don't look like an abstract art exhibition. Unless that's what you're going for.

#21

Nobody Puts Baby in a Corner

Or do we? You'll need several safe places through-out your house to put the baby down. I suggest investing in a baby swing, a portable Pack 'n Play, a stand-up activity center, and a bassinet or crib. Figure out which item is used best in which room. This comes in most handy during bath time. My husband works late, and I usually do dinner/bath/bed solo. If it weren't for the bassi-net in the bathroom, I wouldn't have been able to tackle the routine by myself. Instead, I would've tackled my husband. See? He's alive and well.

#22

Snack Attack

Make sure water and snacks are readily available throughout the day. Especially if you're nursing. Stock up on protein bars, nuts, dried fruit, apples, bananas, oatmeal, string cheese, yogurt, and other healthy snacks. Keep them in your kitchen cabinet, stroller, purse, and car because you'll be eating on the go most of the time. Warning: Your toddler will want to eat what you're eating. Either smarten up and pack enough for two, or learn the fine art of chewing quietly.

#23

Mommy Dates

I love my son. So much so that we are probably a goddamn Freudian case study. The transition from only child to big brother was difficult for both of us. I wasn't sure how I could possibly love this other baby as much as I loved him. But somewhere between all the diaper changes and my sixth bout of mastitis, I fell. Hard. Even so, I missed that one-on-one time. Therefore, we go on "mommy dates." My husband stays home on the weekends with the baby during her morning nap while we get a chance to reconnect. I give my undivided attention and make sure we do something fun together. After an hour or two alone, he is happier, more vocal, and ready to go another twelve rounds with his sister.

#24

My the Force Be with You

If you didn't feel like having sex after one child, you definitely won't feel like it now. You're stressed out, tired, and your bounce back feels more like a slow crawl. It's normal. With that said, sometimes you'll have to force yourself to try. Regardless of how hot your sex life used to be and how much you love your husband, it's different now. You've had an infant on you all day, and your toddler has you on a never-ending emotional rollercoaster. I get it. But if it weren't for *you* two, there wouldn't be *those* two. So make a drink, make an effort, and hell, just make it a quickie.

#25

Stroll Your Roll

I remember back when I was pregnant with my son. My husband and I would be walking through the neighborhood and see families with multiple kids. He would roll his eyes at the toddlers sitting in the stroller and say, "Can't they just walk? They're two!" Well, now our son is that age, and my husband has to push all thirty-three pounds of him down the street. You see, just because they are able to walk doesn't mean they are willing. It also doesn't mean they'll walk in a straight line, follow obediently at your side, or even hold your hand when you ask nicely for the ninth time. Therefore, you get a double stroller. We love the UPPAbaby VISTA. We knew we would most likely have two kids close in age, so we opted for the VISTA when having our first child. It adapts into a double and has various seating options and attachments.

#26

Multitask Like You Mean It

Thought you were good at multitasking before? I did too. But then I wore a sleeping baby while cooking dinner for my toddler that was demanding a cheese stick in a super annoying monster voice with a pore-minimizing mask on my face and trying to catch up with *The Kardashians* in the background as my husband interrupted me for the third time to ask where his shoes were, all the while listening to my mom on the phone as she discussed her luxurious day alone at the nail salon. This. Will. Be. You.

#27

Get Schooled

If you don't have a nanny, reliable daycare, or parents nearby to help, then it's time to think seriously about starting a preschool-type situation at age two. I remember receiving this advice while pregnant with my daughter and sort of brushing it off. Then I gave birth to her, came home, and had my first of many Oh Shit moments. Fast forward six months and we enrolled him in a morning program at age two. I worried nonstop if he was developmentally ready and if this was the right choice. And guess what? Day one at drop off, there was only one of us crying. And it wasn't him. Best decision we ever made.

#28

Use Your Words

As we know, communication in a relationship is important. But when you're sharing household responsibilities with someone while trying to keep two children alive, it becomes crucial. Therefore, use your words. Yes, the same advice you give your toddler, I am giving you. How will he know to empty the dishwasher? Take out the trash? Clean the baby bottles that are sitting next to the sink clearly ready to be washed? You tell him. You give directions. You see, in a perfect world, they know what to do and when to do it without being asked. But in this one, the baby needs to be changed, your toddler is mid-tantrum, and your husband is using this exact moment to ask if he can take a shower. Don't get mad. Get verbal.

#29

It's Not DiGiorno, It's Delivery

Get. Shit. Delivered. There has never been a more convenient time in history to have kids. Between Amazon, Uber Eats, Postmates, Saucey, Instacart, and DoorDash, you never have to leave the house. Unless of course you want to voluntarily suffer through a screaming car ride with two kids just to grab paper towels for the hell of it. In that case, have a psychiatrist delivered. On me.

#30

SOS

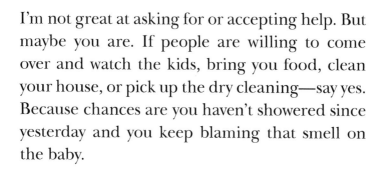

I'm not great at asking for or accepting help. But maybe you are. If people are willing to come over and watch the kids, bring you food, clean your house, or pick up the dry cleaning—say yes. Because chances are you haven't showered since yesterday and you keep blaming that smell on the baby.

#31

Fly Girl

You are going to look like a pack mule walking through the airport. That's OK. Wear the baby in a carrier and put your husband on toddler duty. Pack minimally because you can always buy stuff where you're going. Be organized and put high-use items where you can find them. Bring sanitizer wipes in your carry-on and wipe down surfaces before settling in. Who cares if the old lady next you is rolling her eyes? She doesn't have to play mommy when the kids are sick and your husband has the dreaded man-flu. Also, throw some house rules out the window temporarily. My toddler never used an iPad until our first flight as a family of four. But you know what? I had bigger things to worry about. Like trying to go to the bathroom on an airplane with a sleeping baby strapped to my chest.

#32

Clean Sweep

If you can swing it, hire someone to do a deep clean once a month. You will not believe what can accumulate near the dining table once your baby starts eating solids. In the meantime, buy a lot of disinfecting wipes and scatter them throughout the house. They are easier to grab than a paper towel/spray bottle combo and are better at killing the biological warfare that your toddler is destined to bring home from playdates or preschool.

#33

Nap Time Rewind

There will come a time when their afternoon naps will coincide. Until then, the hardest part of your day is figuring out the baby's sleep schedule and what to do with your toddler in the meantime. It's like a never-ending game of mini-human ping-pong: you put one down as the other one wakes up. Once they do coincide, sit down and relax. I make household duties into a game for my toddler. That way I can catch up on some writing or check out what The Handmaids are doing while they sleep.

#34

The Indoor War

In the early days, I prepared myself for war on a daily basis. If I didn't work out that morning, I would get up five to ten minutes before them and have my coffee. Then I'd throw on my stretchy athleisure armor, mentally prepare myself for defeat, and pray that my son woke up on the right side of the crib that day. Because he is a walking liability, I found it easier if we went to indoor play spaces and children's museums instead of the park. Lucky for me, there aren't any bodies of water, moving cars, or ducks he can chase while running into those moving cars at any of these places. Wear the baby, have fun with your toddler, and drink more coffee.

#35

Wrap It Up

Once you do get your *mojo* back, be careful. Just because you're breastfeeding and haven't had a period since 2016 doesn't mean you aren't primed and ready to get preggers. Talk about contraception and stick to a plan because three under three is *a lot*, and I don't have advice for that shit.

#36

Child labor

I like to clean. My toddler has inherited this genetic predisposition and has started mimicking my actions. Cute, right? Well, I now direct all that cuteness into developmentally appropriate household chores. Whether it's dragging the laundry basket to the washer, tossing his sister's dirty diapers, putting clothes in the hamper, dusting surfaces, cleaning up toys, or rinsing dishes in the sink—he can do it. Next step? Teaching him how to do our taxes and blow-dry my hair.

#37

Weapons of Mass Consumption

When I first had my son, I swore he would never have sweets. I stuck to it for the most part until age two when we ended up using lollipops as weapons on an airplane. Up until then, the poor kid thought raisins were pure gold. So if you're like me and have a stash from last Halloween or Easter, use it for emergencies. This means long car rides, flying, or a very desperate attempt at getting them to sit in the stroller. I'm not suggesting you bribe your child or use sweets on a regular basis. But I sure as shit won't judge if you do. For day-to-day help? Time your toddler's midmorning or midafternoon snack with a stroller walk around the block or to the park. Giving them their apple, string cheese, rice cakes, or smoothie as they sit down makes for an easy transition out the door and into the stroller.

#38

Back That Stash Up

Just because you have a fridge full of prepared meals that are ready to go doesn't mean your toddler will want any of it. Who are we kidding? That chicken you slow roasted and drooled over while cutting into toddler-friendly bites? Gross. The broccoli you carefully steamed so as not to make it too mushy because they like a certain consistency? Not a chance. What to do? Fill up your freezer stash. Stock up on veggie burgers, chicken tenders, sweet potato fries, waffles, a variety of vegetables, and everyone's favorite: pizza. Give two options to your toddler; the more control they have over their environment, the happier they will be.

#39

Routine Queen

I like routine. I like working out in the morning, eating the same predictable, healthy meals, and going to bed around the same time. My son also likes routine. Having a baby sister was a big change for him, and we wanted to stick to his schedule as much as possible. During this transitional time, view your toddler as your constant. I suggest keeping a strict nap and bedtime. Not only do they need the sleep, but you need a predictable end to your day so you can deal with your variable infant.

#40

To Have and to Hold

Kids like to hold shit. No new news here. But now it's twofold, and you're too tired. Make sure there is a toy supply in the car, stroller, and diaper bag. As you know, most kids prefer actual household objects as opposed to toys. That means keys, phones, sunglasses, remotes, and basically anything you're holding. Because they are so close in age, they will most likely want what the other is holding. I noticed this during bath time and bought "neutral territory" toys that they had to share. It works. For now.

Change the Station

The math is easy. Two babies + a shit ton of dia-pers = more changing stations. Have one in each high-use room. Even more if you have multiple levels. The last thing you want to be doing when your baby is mid-blowout is considering your first clean shirt of the day as a legitimate wiping option.

#42

Wanna Spoon?

It goes without saying that every baby is different. My son could have been spoon- and bottle-fed until college. My daughter? Not a chance. Anytime a spoon approached, a swat would soon follow. What to do? Baby-led weaning. I never thought I'd have the patience or ability to not freak out over an array of possible choking hazards, but voilà! She was happy, and I didn't have to purée or test out the techniques learned in our infant CPR class.

#43

Let It GOOOOOO

So, my son likes blondes. But not just any blonde—he likes *the* blonde. Elsa. I'm not sure if it's the tight dress, long hair, or the way she sings so passionately about slamming doors, but hey, that's his choice. One day when coffee-time turned into wine-time, I had one of many not-so-groundbreaking epiphanies: LET IT GO. Like Elsa. What does this mean for a mom of two? Well, let's start with the consistently sticky back seat. Let it go. The ever-present lint on your mom-uniform yoga pants? Let it go. The ring on the coffee table from your husband's water glass? Let it go. The plant that died despite every effort to prove to your mother-in-law you don't have a black thumb? Yeah. Let that shit go. You don't have time to worry about the little stuff. Let alone what your mother-in-law thinks.

#44

Teamwork Makes the Two-under-Two Dream Work

Be a team. You and your husband need to be able to identify strengths and weaknesses in each other. Whatever one lacks, the other makes up. For instance, I am very tidy and clean my house the same way I would clean when turning over an operating room. Quick, efficient, and practically sterile. However, my husband leaves a trail of English muffin crumbs and beard hair wherever he goes. Seriously, if you find the trail, tell him to get his ass home. On the flip side, I can barely use a computer and can't stack a dishwasher to save my life. Thankfully, my husband is basically an iMac with a libido and apparently gets off on dirty dish organization. Who knew?

#45

Opposites Attract

With my son, I loved being pregnant. It was a glowy-skin, manageable-boobs, nap-when-you-need-to kind of situation. By three months, he was sleeping through the night in his own room and naturally weaned himself. I couldn't wait to get pregnant again. With my daughter, I hated being pregnant. I was high risk with a short cervix, had PUPPS for twenty weeks, spent an entire trimester on bed rest, and ate forty pounds' worth of chocolate cake. By eleven months, she finally slept through the night, but I may or may not be nursing her until college drop-off. Now, I *can* wait to get pregnant again. My experiences could not have been more different. So even though you have done this parenting thing before, beware. It may not be the same, and opposites might attract.

My Very Last Bit of Unsolicited Advice

As I sit here putting the finishing touches on my "nonbook book," my daughter is about to turn one. Yes, my daughter, my second born, the living reason I now need eye cream on the daily, is almost a year old. I remember the newborn snuggles, the hours spent nursing, the memories made, and the showers I didn't get the chance to take. And you know what? It was perfect. Not because it was an Instagram-filtered portrayal of parenting, but because it was mine. Tantrums, boo-boos, marital discourse, hormonal sweating, and all. And besides, I don't really know how to use Instagram.

Listen, I'm not going to pretend like I know what the hell I'm doing. Because I don't.

Motherhood is a learn-as-you-go, one-thing-gets-easier-as-something-else-gets-harder, fail-in-order-to-succeed, cry-into-a-nightly-glass-of-wine kind of job. And that's OK. We're OK. Do I hope this helps? Of course. But mostly I just want you to know you're not alone and to try and make you laugh. We take ourselves too seriously and set the bar too high. I know this because my bar is currently orbiting planet Earth somewhere.

But I do know this: parenting two under two is a test of character. Go easy on yourself. Because believe me, they won't. You should take pride in the mundane accomplishments each day. Including that last load of laundry. You should kiss their faces, wash yours more often, and revel in their smallness. And each morning as you start the all-familiar grind of another day, know they are just a little bit older. A little less yours. So remember this phase, Momma. Because not only did you survive, your husband may even still be alive to empty the dishwasher.

About the Author

Danielle is a mom and registered nurse living in Los Angeles with her two babies and toddler husband. She enjoys large cups of coffee, watching *Friends,* and pretending to know how to parent.

Made in the USA
Monee, IL
24 December 2023